D0680081

Canford Cliffs Library
Western Road
Poole BH13 7BN
Tel 01202 707805
Email: canfordclifflibrary@poole.gov.uk

2 8 OCT 2014

1 9 NOV 2014   1 7 AUG 2015   2 6 MAR 2019

08 APR 2019

1 2 JAN 2019 3 0 APR 2019

2 7 FEB 2015   2 3 OCT 2015   2 5 MAY 2019

0 9 FEB 2016 – 7 JUN 2019

1 4 FEB 2015 2 5 JUN 2016

2 0 APR 2015   1 5 JUL 2017   3 0 6 MAR 2020

Please return this item to any Poole library
on or before last date stamped.
Renew on (01202) 265200 or at
www.boroughofpoole.com/libraries

borough of poole.com
1poolelib/0810

BOROUGH OF POOLE

550783856 4

Published by Puffin Books Ltd 2014
A Penguin Company
Penguin Books Ltd, 80 Strand, London, WC2R 0RL, UK
Penguin Group (USA) Inc., 375 Hudson Street, New York 10014, USA
Penguin Books Australia Ltd, 707 Collins Street, Melbourne, Victoria 3008, Australia
Canada, India, New Zealand, South Africa

Written by Barry Hutchison

© 2014 Activision Publishing, Inc. Skylanders Universe is a trademark and Activision is
a registered trademark of Activision Publishing, Inc.

All rights reserved. No part of this publication may be reproduced, stored in a retrieval system,
or transmitted in any form or by any means, electronic, mechanical, photocopying, recording or
otherwise, without the prior consent of the copyright owner.

www.puffinbooks.com

ISBN: 978-0-14135-151-3
001
Printed in China

AIR & EARTH

BOOK OF ELEMENTS

CONTENTS

AIR

EARTH

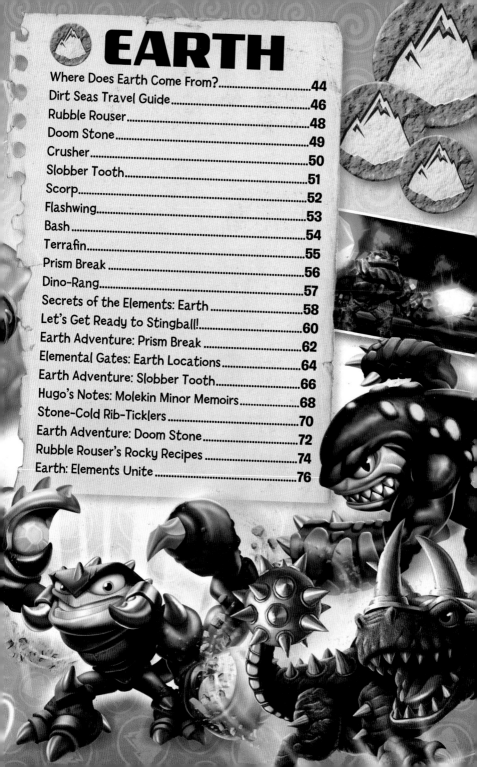

WELCOME!
FROM FLYNN AND HUGO

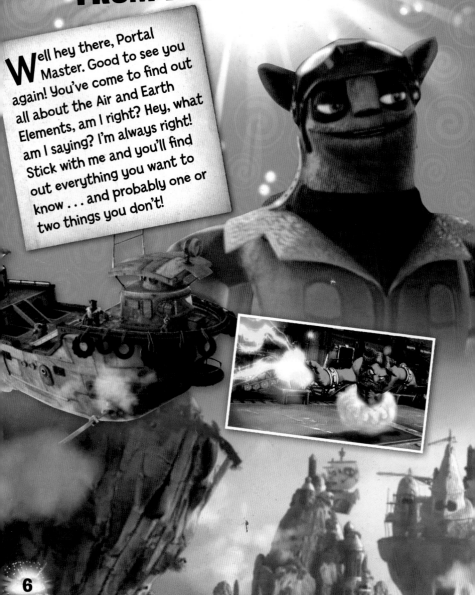

Well hey there, Portal Master. Good to see you again! You've come to find out all about the Air and Earth Elements, am I right? Hey, what am I saying? I'm always right! Stick with me and you'll find out everything you want to know . . . and probably one or two things you don't!

DISCOVER THE MIGHTY POWER OF AIR AND EARTH!

Greetings, seeker of knowledge. There are many nuggets of wisdom I will impart on the following pages. The first of which is: ignore everything Flynn says. He means well, of course, but he doesn't know his Popthorn from his Warnado, so stick with me and I'll open your eyes to all the wonders of the Earth and Air elements.

WHERE DOES AIR COME FROM?

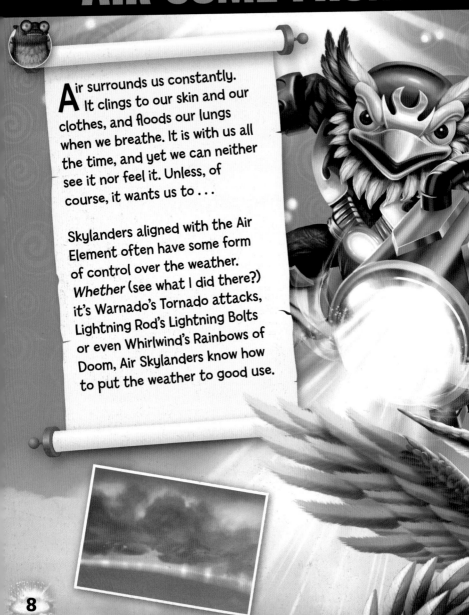

Air surrounds us constantly. It clings to our skin and our clothes, and floods our lungs when we breathe. It is with us all the time, and yet we can neither see it nor feel it. Unless, of course, it wants us to . . .

Skylanders aligned with the Air Element often have some form of control over the weather. *Whether* (see what I did there?) it's Warnado's Tornado attacks, Lightning Rod's Lightning Bolts or even Whirlwind's Rainbows of Doom, Air Skylanders know how to put the weather to good use.

What's more, the skies above, around – and often below – Skylands are infinite, meaning the Air Element may well hold a limitless number of secrets we're not yet aware of. This makes the Air Element one of the most mysterious of them all!

THE AIR SKYLANDERS ATTACK LIKE A BOLT FROM THE BLUE!

WICKED WEATHER

As I mentioned, the Air Element is largely responsible for some of Skylands' more . . . unusual weather patterns. I don't think anyone would have been able to forecast some of these outbreaks.

THE GREAT BLACK WHIRL STORM

Many years ago, Master Eon compiled a long, detailed report on the Great Black Whirl Storm. Unfortunately, it blew away the moment he finished writing it, so all we have to go on now is rumour and hearsay.

What we do know is that the Great Black Whirl Storm claimed the lives of dozens of explorers way back in . . . um, whenever it happened. We have good reason to believe the storm was black and whirly. It was also great, although it should be stressed that it was great in the "big" sense, rather than the "this is terrific" sense.

LIGHTNING

Most of the lightning bolts that split the sky in Skylands have been hurled by Storm Titans. Competitive by nature, Storm Titans are constantly trying to prove they're greater than each other. This can result in some pretty spectacular light shows.

Sometimes they get a little carried away, like Lightning Rod did when he misjudged a throw and burned a watching cyclops to a crisp. Well, it's one way to shock the audience!

ANVIL RAIN

Bringing a whole new meaning to the phrase "heavy shower", Skylanders have often summoned a downpour of Anvil Rain to help smash the forces of Kaos to squidgy lumps.

With the simplest of incantations, a skilled Skylander can cause dozens of heavy iron anvils to plummet from the sky for anything up to forty-five seconds. No umbrella in the world is going to stand up to that!

ENCHANTED TWISTER

Sometimes, the weather in Skylands can be so powerful that it transforms the ordinary into the extraordinary. Take the Skylander Warnado, for instance. He was destined to be nothing more than your average, run-of-the-mill swamp turtle. That is until, while still in his egg, he was lifted into the air by an enchanted twister.

Not only did the twister spin him around a bit - it actually raised him, teaching him the windy ways that made him the powerful Skylander he is today. So watch out for wind!

BOOM JET

FACTFILE

- Highly-skilled sky-surfer
- His bombs can prove a nasty surprise to villains below
- A bit of a show-off. OK, a LOT of a show-off
- Used his flying skills to save his home town from the Darkness

DID YOU KNOW?

Even as a child, Boom Jet was a thrill-seeker who was always climbing up things, then throwing himself head-first off them. It wasn't until he fitted his shoes with rockets when he was six years old, though, that Boom Jet's career as a daredevil really took off. He immediately crashed through a wall, but he tried and tried again and is now considered one of the greatest sky-surfers of all time.

90%

AIR RATING

FREE RANGER

FACTFILE

- Hatched in a raging thunderstorm
- Loves to chase storms and throw himself into them
- Incredibly brave (but also a big chicken)
- Pecks lumps out of evil

DID YOU KNOW?

There can be few births more traumatic than having your egg smashed open by a bolt of lightning - but that's exactly how Free Ranger entered the world. The *egg*-splosion ignited his love of bad weather, and led to a lifetime of chasing down horrendous hurricanes, terrible twisters and doom-laden drizzle. On the flip-side, he's also been known to feel uncomfortable in confined spaces, making him rubbish at hide-and-seek.

AIR RATING

93%

SWARM

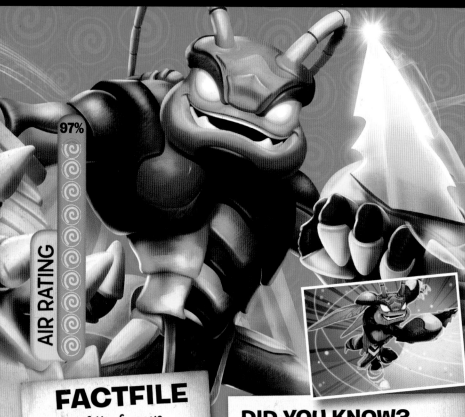

AIR RATING 97%

FACTFILE

- One of the famous Skylanders Giants
- A REALLY big bug
- Has almost nine thousand stripy siblings
- Prince of a proud people

DID YOU KNOW?

Having nearly nine thousand brothers and sisters means that when Swarm isn't battling the forces of evil, he has to spend a lot of his time writing birthday cards and wrapping presents. While this is a lot of work for one insect to do (even a Giant), it does mean that on his own birthday he receives an enormous pile of gifts.

POP THORN

FACTFILE

- A member of the Pufferthorn race
- Hates being used as a comb
- Looks cute, but is far from cuddly
- Can be prickly to deal with

AIR RATING

64%

DID YOU KNOW?

Soon after Pop Thorn was born, the Pufferthorns held a competition to find the cutest baby. The entries were all so adorable that every single one of them tied for first place. Except, that is, for Pop Thorn, who came second. Even back then, it seems, there was a hint of danger about him that was not present in other Pufferthorns.

SCRATCH

78%

AIR RATING

FACTFILE

- Her razor-sharp claws can leave a nasty scratch
- Customized armour gives her an edge in battle
- Has an incredible sense of balance
- Was introduced to the Skylanders by none other than Jet-Vac

DID YOU KNOW?

When pirate Greebles arrived in a fleet of airships to attack young Scratch's home, they got a lot more than they bargained for. Scratch put her fighting skills to good use, in a battle that raged across the skies for days on end. It was also on this fateful occasion that she discovered enormous airships really don't cope very well with razor-sharp claws.

JET-VAC

FACTFILE

- One of the most daring flying aces of all time
- Sacrificed his wings to save a mother and her children
- Flies with the aid of a jet-powered vacuum device
- One of the noblest of all the Skylanders

DID YOU KNOW?

As well as using it to fight the minions of Kaos and the Darkness, Jet-Vac has been known to use his Vac Blaster to help out with odd jobs around the place, like clearing away leaves, lifting crumbs off the carpet and blowing away Flame Imps who try any of their mischief.

AIR RATING

◎◎◎◎◎◎◎◎◎◎ **71%**

SONIC BOOM

FACTFILE

- Tough griffin momma
- Her cunning and bravery are legendary
- Keeps her kids with her at all times
- Causes splitting headaches for evildoers

70%

AIR RATING

DID YOU KNOW?

Disaster almost befell Sonic Boom and her hatchlings when Ghost Roaster decided to whip up a batch of pancakes. She caught the spooky chef just as he was about to crack one of her eggs into a mixing bowl. Needless to say she wasn't happy, and poor Ghost Roaster didn't know what hit him!

LIGHTNING ROD

FACTFILE

- The most macho of all the Storm Titans
- The most famous, too!
- Can bench-press 250 tons
- Has a best-selling autobiography, titled 'Rod the Bod'

DID YOU KNOW?

When he isn't taking part in grand lightning-hurling tournaments or battling evil, Lightning Rod can usually be found posing for sculptors. At the last count there were over two thousand statues of him dotted around the Cloud Kingdom - all exactly the same.

AIR RATING

 72%

WHIRLWIND

68%

AIR RATING

FACTFILE

- Unicorn-dragon hybrid
- Incredibly graceful in the air
- Can be a bit moody sometimes
- Shoots rainbows from her unicorn horn

DID YOU KNOW?

When Whirlwind first revealed that one of her attacks was called the Rainbow of Doom, Flynn laughed. That was his first mistake. His second mistake was not running away fast enough. Still, he was back on his feet after just a few weeks, so at least Whirlwind went easy on him.

WARNADO

FACTFILE

- Hatched inside a magical twister
- Gets dizzy when standing still
- Tough shell makes him a hard nut to crack
- Summons tornadoes to aid him in battle

DID YOU KNOW?

Having grown up inside an enchanted tornado, Warnado finds it hard to keep his feet on the ground. When he and Eruptor stumbled upon a travelling fairground during one particular adventure, Warnado couldn't believe his luck. It's fair to say that the strangely pale-looking Eruptor didn't enjoy those twenty-seven turns on the roller coaster quite as much as Warnado did!

AIR RATING

⊚ ⊚ ⊚ ⊚ ⊚ ⊚ ⊚ ⊚ ⊚ ⊚ **63%**

SECRETS OF THE ELEMENTS:
AIR

Air is a far-reaching and mysterious Element indeed. As you'd imagine for a place called Skylands, we've got rather a lot of sky. It's everywhere!

Except on the ground.

Yes, except on the ground. Thank you, Flynn. That was very helpful.

And in the sea.

Right, yes. There's no sky in the sea, either. Thank you for that.

No problem.

Please be quiet, Flynn! Sorry. Where was I? Oh yes, the sky. There's really rather a lot of it, and here are just some of the things you might find there.

FROM HERE TO AIR

Air Skylanders are able to use some pretty impressive ways of getting from A to B. Sure, there are the obvious ones like flying (Whirlwind), sky-surfing (Boom Jet) or, er, jet-vacking (Jet-Vac). But they also have their own unique way of journeying through Elemental Gates. When they reach an Air gate, they summon a swirly cyclone of wind that spirits them through to whatever terrain awaits.

GHOST SHIPS

These ghostly galleons are cursed to roam the skies forever, usually with crews made up of nasty spooks and spirits. While strong in the Undead Element, these vessels also make use of Air to propel themselves creepily through the skies. Shudder!

Legend says that if you cross paths with a ghost ship it will give chase, and will not stop until it catches you and adds you to its cadaverous crew. Then again, legend also says that Flynn is the best pilot in Skylands (see below), so you can't believe everything you hear.

FLYNN

Yes, it seems that no matter where you go you can't get away from Flynn. Whether it's in his hot air balloon or that ghastly flying ship, the Dread-Yacht, he can usually be found floating around somewhere up there in the skies. The Air Element has been kind to him over the years, in as much as it's allowed him to fly clumsily around without smashing himself into tiny bits. As I mentioned above, there is a rumour that Flynn is the greatest pilot in all of Skylands. It's worth noting that the person spreading these rumours is almost certainly Flynn himself.

UP, UP AND AWAY!
WITH JET-VAC

The Sky Baron, Jet-Vac, must surely be among the most noble of all the Skylanders. Which is saying something, because they're really rather a noble bunch. Despite having no wings, he's a real flying ace. Here, he kindly shares with us his great knowledge, along with some practical advice.

HOW TO FLY

So, a little birdie tells me you'd like to be a pilot, eh? Good show! Anyone can learn to fly, but it takes a special kind of character to be able to soar, if you know what I mean. Here are some tips to help get your head in the clouds . . .

1. Get off the ground. Probably the most important lesson of all, this one. The ground is not in the least bit suitable for flying on. If you're on the ground then you're doing the precise opposite of flying, and that's no use at all.

2. Get out of the water. As above. You may be able to float in water, but that won't help you to fly.

101 Uses for Jet-Vac's Jet Pack
61. Cooling food that's just come out of the oven.

3. Get into the air. Now that's more like it! You see that wide open space above you? That's the sky. Get yourself into it using any means you have at your disposal.

4. Stay there.

5. Congratulations! You can now fly. Chocks away!

FLYING LINGO

Being able to fly is all well and good, but if you want to be a real pilot you have to learn to talk like one. It's a bit of a complex code, so pay attention.

101 Uses for Jet-Vac's Jet Pack
42. Winning at blow football.

Chocks away! = Ready for take-off!

Tally-ho! = I have spotted the enemy and am preparing to engage, *or* Race you to the corner and back!

Hedge-hopping = Flying dangerously low.

Old bean = A good friend.

Chompies at twelve o'clock = I've forgotten to pack a parachute!

Let's go bomb Kaos = Pop the kettle on, I'll be home in twenty minutes.

101 Uses for Jet-Vac's Jet Pack
87. Blowing up balloons at children's parties.

AAAAAAARGH! = I believe I am about to crash.

Send urgent medical attention = I have crashed.

A BRUSH WITH DANGER

FLYNN'S FABLES

Trolls. Don't you just love 'em?

Nah, probably not. And I don't blame you. Those brutes can be real nasty. I mean, I could take one down if I wanted to, but they smell absolutely terrible! That's why I run away screaming whenever I see one. It's not because I'm scared or anything, and anyone who says otherwise is a liar.

Someone else who didn't enjoy the scent of troll is Pop Thorn. Like most Pufferthorns, Pop Thorn spent his days puffing around looking all cute and adorable, and his nights being dragged across a troll's filthy scalp.

You see, troll hair is too tangled for ordinary combs to deal with, so the lumbering oafs took to using Pufferthorns

to brush out the tugs. I don't know why they bothered. I mean, no hairstyle in the world is going to make a troll look good, you know what I'm saying? Even I couldn't make those guys look attractive, and if there's anyone who knows about being super-handsome it's me.

Anyway, every night some big troll would snatch up the closest Pufferthorn and spend several minutes yanking the poor thing's spikes through their horrible troll hair. One night, Pop Thorn decided he had had enough.

Everyone knows that trolls love blowing stuff up, but Pop Thorn could blow something up, too – himself. As soon as the troll picked him up, Pop Thorn inflated and pushed his spikes out as far as they would go. The troll yelped in pain and tried to drop him, but Pop Thorn rolled up the troll's shoulder, down its back and . . . well, let's just say he stuck those spikes into a very tender area.

Word soon spread that there was at least one Pufferthorn who fought back, and soon after the trolls abandoned brushing their hair for good. Way to go Pop Thorn, you little cutie-pie, you!

ELEMENTAL GATES: AIR LOCATIONS

Located throughout Skylands are a number of gates that can only be opened by Skylanders aligned with the Air Element. Beyond these gates lie all manner of secrets and surprises. Here are a few located in and around the Cloudbreak Islands that you may not know about...

MOUNT CLOUDBREAK

Cross the bridge in Old Treetop Terrace and then turn left to find an Air Gate. Hop through and get ready to show off your shooting skills. Hit all the targets and you'll be the proud owner of a Winged Sapphire.

HARD

ACCESS OF LOCATION

EASY

IRON JAW GULCH

After destroying the first airship you'll land near a gate that requires both the Air and Tech Elements to open it. This looks like a job for a SWAP Force Skylander! Or possibly two regular Skylanders working as a team. There's a very stylish hat waiting within.

ACCESS OF LOCATION

HARD

EASY

FROSTFEST MOUNTAINS

At Ice Break Atolls, hop across the blocks of ice floating in the river to find an Air Gate just waiting to be opened. Be careful though – that water looks freezing! Clear the course beyond the gate and claim your prize!

ACCESS OF LOCATION

EASY

HARD

FLYNN'S FABLES

SOAR UP, PIPE DOWN

Back before Master Eon recruited him to the ranks of the Skylanders, Boom Jet lived for just one thing – speed and danger. (That's two things – Hugo).

The problem was, some of his neighbours had to get up for work in the morning, and they didn't take too kindly to him roaring about with his jet engine at all hours of the night. They complained, and for a while it looked like Boom Jet's night training was over.

That is until he came up with an idea so brilliant it could have been one of mine. One evening, just before it got dark, he fired up his engine and zoomed high into the sky. Then, so as not to disturb the people sleeping below, he did something really unexpected.

He turned the engine off. I know, pretty crazy, right?

Well it turns out gravity thought so too, and he immediately began to fall. But being the experienced sky-surfer that he is, Boom Jet was able to turn his powerless sky sled into a glider.

Some say he bounced on the clouds themselves. Others say he put string round birds and used them to pull him along. The only person who really knows for sure what went down that night is Boom Jet, and when you ask him about it all he does is smile and look wistfully up to the sky.

At least, I'm guessing that's where he's looking. It's not easy to tell with those goggles.

HUGO'S NOTES

AIRY BEASTS

There's an old children's rhyme in Skylands that includes the line, "there's none so fair as beasts of Air". The poem also rhymes "magic" with "tragic" and says that "those of Undead have a bulbuous head", so while it's very popular in some places, it doesn't go down nearly so well in others.

Anyway, I thought I'd take this opportunity to tell you about some of those fair – and not so fair – creatures of the Skylands Air.

SKY BARONS

The Sky Barons are a race of proud warrior folk who are like eagles in almost all respects but one – they are born without wings. In keeping with their traditions, Sky Barons are given magical wings when they are young, allowing them to master flying at a very early age.

The most famous of all the Sky Barons is Jet-Vac, who sacrificed his wings to help others, and in doing so drew the attention of a certain bearded Portal Master, who recruited him to join the Skylanders.

SKY PIRATES

It's not easy to explain what Sky Pirates are. They're sort of like normal pirates, only in the sky. Actually, that was quite easy after all.

As with water-based pirates, Sky Pirates range from the truly evil to the vaguely annoying. They love nothing more than swooping down in their airships, cannons blasting, then swiping anything they can get their hands on. They love to steal treasure, but if there's no treasure available they'll pinch anything from exotic fruit to unusually shaped rocks. They just can't get enough of stealing.

LITTLE BIRDS

We've all seen them fluttering around Skylands. They zip about while Spyro toasts trolls, flap around while Terrafin pummels cyclopses and hover in the background as Warnado clobbers Kaos. They tweet and chirp and generally make the place seem a little nicer.

There are many species of Skylands bird, from the common Lesser-Headed Warbler, to the ever-so-rare Purple Snerp. They never ask for anything or cause any problems (except when they chirp outside Eruptor's window early in the morning). I, for one, think Skylands is a better place for having them (except for the one that keeps doing its droppings on my head when I least expect it - I'm not keen on him at all).

THE BATTLE OF CAT'S EYE MOUNTAIN

Situated high in the towering peaks of Cat's Eye Mountain stands one of the most spectacular cities in all of Skylands. Built entirely of crystal and gold, this sparkling metropolis was a safe haven to all who lived there, as it could only be accessed by creatures of the Air Element.

That all changed when a gang of Pirate Greebles turned up in their fleet of flying warships. They had come to plunder the city of its riches, and with their cannons blasting and their cutlasses slicing, they brought much of the city to its knees.

All looked to be lost, until a winged cat-creature named Scratch decided to fight back. Equipped with a suit of enchanted armour, some sharp claws and a really nasty temper, Scratch showed those invading pirates exactly what she thought of them.

For days she swiped and slashed and battled against them. Although she was fast and powerful, the sheer number of villains threatened to overwhelm Scratch. Until, that is, she realized their airships were built around enormous balloons.

A few carefully aimed claw slashes later, and the pirates were sent plummeting back down to earth. From that day to this, no Greeble has dared return to Cat's Eye Mountain, and the city is safe once more.

SCRATCH'S ARMOUR

It's not every day you see a cat wearing a metal mask and matching gloves, but then again Scratch is no everyday moggy. As well as helping to protect her in the heat of battle, the narrow eyes and pointed teeth of the mask prove very handy when it comes to terrifying everyone she meets.

The crystal claws of her gauntlets are able to cut through virtually any substance, from solid rock to hardened steel, meaning there are very few enemies who can stand up to a scratching from Scratch.

FLYNN'S FABLES

FREE RANGER'S WINDY DAY

If there's one thing Free Ranger loves, it's wind – and I don't mean the kind I got when I accidently ate one of Camo's chili peppers. Cali wouldn't come near me for days. At least, not without holding her nose.

But I'm getting off-topic. The kind of winds that get Free Ranger excited are tornadoes and twisters and all the others that can sweep you up and carry you off to who-knows-where.

Now, most sensible folks would run away from an oncoming whirlwind, but not Free Ranger. That chicken is no chicken, and instead of running away he runs towards them and hurls himself right into the middle!

Usually he does this for fun, but one time he had a much better reason for risking his neck, when he spotted a tornado heading straight towards a group of helpless Mabu.

Those little guys were up on a hillside enjoying a picnic, when along came the swirliest, twirliest twister they'd ever set eyes on. First, their snacks were sucked in by the spinning wind. Then their blanket. And then their basket.

The Mabu tried to run, but those stumpy little legs of theirs were getting them nowhere. Luckily for them, Free Ranger had been following the storm closely, and when he saw the Mabu were in trouble he dived right on in. Through sheer strength of will,

and probably also some fancy wing-work, Free Ranger was able to steer the storm away from the Mabu, saving the day. How amazing is that? The guy wrestled with a tornado and won! As a thank you, the Mabu presented Free Ranger with a picnic hamper full of food. Which was handy, because he was feeling really peckish. Get it? PECK-ish! Because he's a chicken! Man, I crack myself up sometimes.

PUFFERTHORN PREENING

Having spent many years as a hair care product, Pop Thorn knows a thing or two about personal grooming. Here he shares his dos and don'ts for looking good.

DO
keep fit by running around outdoors.

DON'T
run face-first into a rock golem. That won't help.

DO
eat healthily.
A balanced diet makes your skin look great.

DON'T
smear food all over your face in the hope it'll work faster.

DO
brush your teeth twice a day.

DON'T
use a brick to do it

DO
smile and try to look friendly.

DON'T
overdo it or people will think you're crazy.

DO
bathe regularly.

DON'T
do it in a lava pool.

TROLL HAIR CARE

Since deciding that Pufferthorns were just too dangerous to comb their hair with, the giant trolls have tried several other methods of keeping their locks under control. Not being the most intelligent of creatures, some of the items the trolls have attempted to brush with have been unusual to say the least. Some of the worst include:

- Twigs
- Rocks
- Flame Imps
- Pirate cutlasses
- Flynn
- Sand
- Other trolls
- Shoes
- Water
- Four unicorns tied to a stick
- Jelly

AIR:
ELEMENTS UNITE

The vast and mysterious Air Element combines with the others in a number of interesting and unusual ways.

WEAKNESS

While the Air Element is strong when facing the Earth Element, it is much less able to deal with Fire. Air Skylanders must be extra careful when facing Fire-powered enemies.

HOW AIR ENTWINES WITH THE OTHER ELEMENTS

EARTH
Air's winds help sculpt and shape the Earth

FIRE
The oxygen in Air adds fuel to the Fire

LIFE
Wind brings rain, and rain makes Life grow

MAGIC
Inflates Magic's power to dizzying new heights

TECH
Lightning bolts give Tech a real charge

UNDEAD
Thunder acts as the Undead's ominous fanfare

WATER
Strong winds make for bigger waves

AIR
SKYLANDERS

LIGHTNING ROD

WARNADO

WHIRLWIND

JET-VAC

POP THORN

SONIC BOOM

SCRATCH

EARTH
SKYLANDERS

PRISM BREAK

BASH

FLASHWING

TERRAFIN

SCORP

DINO-RANG

SLOBBER TOOTH

43

WHERE DOES EARTH COME FROM?

What does Earth make us think of? Rocks . . . soil . . . dry, dusty landscapes . . . feeling really, really, thirsty?

Perhaps, but the Earth Element has much more to it than that, and Skylanders who draw on its power are a real force to be reckoned with. Whether causing earthquakes, projecting energy beams through crystal, or swimming through rock, Earth Skylanders have all manner of tricks at their disposal for battling evil. Start a fight with an Earth Skylander, and it's almost like you're starting a fight with Skylands itself.

Even now, we have only just begun to explore the vast and mysterious world beneath our feet. Many of the creatures aligned with Earth are rare and fantastic beasts, from Rock Golems to Dirt Sharks. And, with so much of our underground world still undiscovered, I suspect there are plenty of other strange specimens where those came from. I, for one, can't wait to see what crawls free from the soil.

EARTH SKYLANDERS ARE AT ONE WITH THE GROUND ITSELF!

DIRT SEAS TRAVEL GUIDE

SO YOU'RE OFF TO THE DIRT SEAS?

You've booked your tickets. You've packed your bags. Your friends and family think you've lost your mind, and you probably have. But you don't care – you're off on the holiday of a lifetime (probably not in a good way) to the Dirt Seas! Here's how to get the most out of your trip!

Squeeze in as much as you can with the help of our daily planner . . .

MONDAY: Check in to your hotel. For this you will need a spade, a bucket and enough energy to dig continuously for several hours in the blazing sunshine.

TUESDAY: Get up early. Apply cream to your sunburn. Sob uncontrollably and shout "DON'T TOUCH ME!" at anyone who comes within five metres. Hallucinate about a big fish calling you names. Go back to bed.

WEDNESDAY: Drink several litres of water in one go. Venture outside. Look at some rocks. Shrug. Go back inside.

THURSDAY: Look at some other rocks. Poke the ground with a stick (must supply own stick). Mutter something about never using that travel agent again. Go back inside.

FRIDAY: Walk for miles in any random direction. Look at some rocks. Realize you have no idea where your hotel is and spend the next twelve hours trying to retrace your steps.

The Dirt Seas were once home to Terrafin, and a popular Skylands holiday resort to boot. Sadly, the whole area was turned into glass by a massive explosion, but my research has uncovered this extract from an old travel guide. It gives us an idea of what life there was once like . . .

SATURDAY: Go outside. Briefly imagine you see something interesting in the distance, then realize it was a trick of the light. Kick a stone. Go back inside. Cry yourself to sleep.

SUNDAY: Leave the hotel and vow to never come back, before spending several hours filling in the hole you made on Monday as the sun relentlessly blisters the skin on your shoulders and neck.

THINGS TO BRING WHEN VISITING THE DIRT SEAS

- Water
- Sun cream
- A big hat
- More water

THINGS NOT TO BRING WHEN VISITING THE DIRT SEAS

- Sand
- Rocks
- A big hat with a magnifying glass mounted on the top

RUBBLE ROUSER

EARTH RATING

89%

FACTFILE

- Used to eat rock for a living
- Teeth are as hard as diamonds (but not as shiny)
- Loves to try out any new tool
- Villains get a real kick out of his drill feet

DID YOU KNOW?

Rubble Rouser once tried to win a cuddly toy on a Test-Your-Strength attraction. He paid his money, took aim with his hammer, then slammed it against the base of the machine. Instead of ringing the bell at the top, though, the blow smashed the machine to pieces and triggered a minor earthquake. Rubble Rouser never did get that teddy bear.

DOOM STONE

EARTH RATING

94%

FACTFILE

- Carved from the strongest stone in all of Skylands
- Brought to life by a wizard
- Good at fetching and carrying heavy objects
- His armour makes him virtually indestructible

DID YOU KNOW?

The wizard who brought Doom Stone to life was incredibly lazy. As well as getting Doom Stone to do all the heavy lifting around his house, the wizard also once set him the task of washing all his windows. Unfortunately, Doom Stone's super-strength squeegee skills meant every window shattered to pieces at his slightest touch. The wizard vowed from that day forth to always use a professional window cleaner.

CRUSHER

FACTFILE

- One of the fabled Skylanders Giants
- Loves crushing rocks
- Loves crushing evil even more
- Can freeze enemies with his goggles

DID YOU KNOW?

Crusher has the ability to self-destruct at will. This can be useful during battle, but at other times it's something of a nuisance Once, while patrolling near a Mabu village, Crusher sneezed. The resulting explosion sent his body parts flying in several different direction and took out half of th houses in the village.

98%

EARTH RATING

SLOBBER TOOTH

FACTFILE

- Has some serious teeth. Just look at them!

- Lay in hibernation for thousands of years

- Shunned a job offer from Kaos

- Gruff and headstrong

DID YOU KNOW?

It takes Slobber Tooth almost an hour a day to keep his teeth in tip-top condition. This is partly because his fangs are so large and prominent, and partly because it's quite difficult to hold a toothbrush with those hands. Or claws. Or whatever they are.

EARTH RATING

79%

SCORP

76%

EARTH RATING

FACTFILE

- Grew up on the Salt Flat Islands
- Winner of several Stingball championships
- Loves hot, dry weather conditions
- Powerful claws defeat enemies in a snip

DID YOU KNOW?

Scorp likes to sleep underground, or beneath large rocks. Once, after a hard day of battling evil, he curled up under a boulder to have a nap. He didn't realize, though, that the boulder was actually one of Crusher's feet. It was only Scorp's tough armoured body that saved him from being squished flat!

FLASHWING

71%

EARTH RATING

DID YOU KNOW?

Flashwing is one of the most stunning-looking of all the Skylanders, and she knows it! She once arranged a beauty contest that was open to male and female Skylanders alike. However, as well as entering the contest, she appointed herself as judge. Needless to say she didn't just take first place . . . she took second and third, too!

FACTFILE

- Loves to be in the spotlight
- Her past is a mystery
- Shoots laser pulses from her tail
- Hatched from a giant geode

BASH

67%

EARTH RATING

FACTFILE

- Dreams of being able to fly
- Despite having no wings, he's technically a dragon
- Armoured shell and spikes protect him from danger
- Appears mean and moody, but he's sensitive deep down

DID YOU KNOW?

Over the years, Bash has made several attempts at flying, despite having no wings. He has jumped off high cliffs, leaped from airships and even launched himself into the sky from a giant catapult. He always makes a painful landing, but he refuses to give up and insists that one day he'll soar like the other dragons.

TERRAFIN

FACTFILE

- Loves a really good battle, especially in the ring
- Can swim beneath the ground
- His powerful jaws can chomp through hard stone
- Brass knuckles deliver knockout blows to his enemies

DID YOU KNOW?

Terrafin might be one of the toughest of all the Skylanders, but there's one thing he's afraid of - flying! To get him into Flynn's balloon, Master Eon used to cast a spell to send him into a gentle sleep, before the other Skylanders would carry him on board. Mind you, with the way Flynn flies that thing, it's no wonder Terrafin was worried.

EARTH RATING

69%

PRISM BREAK

FACTFILE

- Was trapped underground for a century
- Boasts arms made of solid crystal
- Can fire bolts of pure energy
- Deeply serious, and rarely cracks a smile

DID YOU KNOW?

One year, on Trigger Happy's birthday, a sudden downpour of rain ruined a surprise fireworks display Spyro had arranged. Everyone was disappointed, but Prism Break had an idea. He had Whirlwind shoot out a rainbow from her horn, then used his prism arms to bend the colours in all different directions. The resulting light show was truly incredible, and Trigger Happy had the best birthday ever!

74%

EARTH RATING

DINO-RANG

61%

EARTH RATING

FACTFILE

- A dinosaur - definitely not a dragon
- Cool and calm in a crisis
- Fights evil with his deadly Stone Boomerangs
- Comes from a mysterious land far, far away

DID YOU KNOW?

Despite his size, Dino-Rang is a surprisingly gifted dancer. Sometimes, though, he forgets his own strength. Once, when dancing with a female partner, he attempted to lift her above his head, and accidentally launched her screaming several miles into the air. She has not, as of yet, come back down.

SECRETS OF THE ELEMENTS:
EARTH

If any Element is likely to leave you shaking in your shoes (literally), it's Earth and its ground-trembling earthquakes. Even so, it's very easy to take Earth for granted. After all, it's just there all the time, sort of lying around not doing very much. A bit like Flynn, now I come to think about it.

Hey, I heard that!

But there's much more to Earth than meets the eye . . .

NURTURING SOIL

Earth's soil may look very much like a lot of old dirt with some lumps in, but without it Skylands would be a desolate and unforgiving place. All plants and trees owe their existence to the soil, from the tiniest saplings all the way up to the Tree of Life. Although the Giant, Tree Rex, is aligned with the Life Element, without Earth's soil he would never have existed in the first place.

STEADFAST AND SOLID

All Skylanders are tough, but Earth Skylanders are among the toughest of the lot. Those who aren't cut from living rock, generally tend to be equipped with stony shells or diamond-hard armour. One of the few exceptions to this rule is Terrafin, and yet his skin is tough enough to withstand swimming through densely-packed dirt and rock.

PRECIOUS STONES

Not all the rocks buried beneath Skylands are of the grey and brown variety. The ground plays host to all manner of precious gems, many of which possess mysterious powers. Decades spent trapped underground turned Prism Break's hands into stunning crystals, which he now uses to clobber enemies into submission.

Perhaps the most precious stones of all are Soul Gems. These beautiful purple rocks each contain a very special secret. Any Skylander who finds one can draw on its magic and use it to learn a new ability. It's no wonder Soul Gems have become such a vital weapon in the battle against the Darkness!

LET'S GET READY TO STINGBALL!

Back when he lived on the Salt Flat Islands, Scorp was a champion at the sport of Stingball. In fact, he was so good at it that he was crowned The King of Sting more times than any other player in the history of the game. Stingball is something of a - how can I put this - extreme game, and only the bravest (or, sometimes, stupidest) dare take part. Don't believe me? Just take a look at my research into the sport.

STINGBALL RULES

The aim of the game is to smash the ball into your opponents' faces as fast and as hard as possible. The ball (in actual fact, a vaguely round boulder) must be struck using a player's claws or stinger only. Should the ball hit the ground before thumping into an opposing player's face, the striking player must consume his or her own weight in sand before play can continue.

The winning team is the one whose players aren't all lying face-down on the ground unconscious, covered in bruises and with no teeth left.

SOME POINTS TO NOTE:

1. No crying. Anyone caught crying, weeping, sobbing or even looking slightly moist around the eyes will be forcibly removed from the playing arena and hurled off a cliff.

2. No violence. Ha-ha, just kidding! Violence is positively encouraged.

3. Ducking, dodging or otherwise avoiding the ball is not permitted. Take what's coming to you, and don't be a wimp.

STINGBALL MOVES

The following techniques should be studied and learned in order to become a true Stingball master:

The Jaw Shatter
The Hurtling Thud
The Brick Chew
The Flying Brick Chew (advanced)
The Sliding Ooyah
New Knees Please
The Ambulance

CURRENT LEAGUE STANDINGS

Team Name	W	D	L	Points
The Brutes	5	1	0	16
Face Smashers United	5	0	1	15
Salt Flat Rangers	2	1	3	7
Walking Wounded SC	1	0	4	3
Look Ma, No Teeth	0	0	5	0

HOOKING UP WITH PRISM BREAK

FLYNN'S FABLES

Although Prism Break and I are great friends, our relationship got off to a bit of a rocky start (Get it? Man, I'm funny!) way back when we first met.

I'm the type of guy who's always on the lookout for an opportunity, and one time I was flying around in my balloon when I spotted these two enormous diamonds just lying around on a rock!

I was able to slow my balloon down by skillfully crashing it into a tree, but there wasn't enough room to come down to land, so I decided to try hooking the diamonds with my anchor.

As luck would have it, I'm pretty talented at hooking things with that anchor, and it took only twenty or thirty attempts before I managed to snare one of the diamonds! What can I say? I'm a talented guy.

The problem was, a diamond that size was too heavy even for me. So I decided to take the balloon higher and pull the diamond along beneath it until I found somewhere else to land.

Like I say, that was one heavy gemstone, and it took almost all my fuel to get the balloon to lift into the air. It was only when

I'd cleared the treetops that I heard the angry shout from the end of the anchor chain.

As it turned out, those diamonds were actually Prism Break's crystal arms. He was having a break after smashing up some Trollverines and had fallen asleep. You'd think he would have been grateful that I woke him up before anyone tried a sneak attack, but he really wasn't.

We're tight these days, of course. But Prism Break never lets me forget that day we first met!

ELEMENTAL GATES:
EARTH LOCATIONS

I've already mentioned the Air Elemental Gates, but did you know there are Earth Elemental Gates waiting to be opened, too? Oh . . . you did? Right. Well here are a few places around the Cloudbreak Islands where you can find just a few of them.

CASCADE GLADE

The gate you'll find in the Gobblepod Sanctuary area of Cascade Glade is a little different. It can only be opened by both Earth and Tech Elements working together. Either a SWAP Force Skylander with both Elements, or two Skylanders working together can open it up to claim the treasure waiting inside.

ACCESS OF LOCATION

HARD

EASY

BONEY ISLANDS

Near Glacial Gallery is a flaming bridge. Take a left just before it and you'll find one of the gates just waiting to be opened. Beyond it lies three Battle Gates, lots of villainous types, and – if you survive – a precious Winged Sapphire.

ACCESS OF LOCATION

HARD

EASY

KAOS' FORTRESS

Deep in the fortress you'll come across the spinning blades of the Chompie Churners. Head down to one of these horrible contraptions then leap from the blade onto a small dirt path. You'll find an Earth gate waiting, with a diabolical challenge inside.

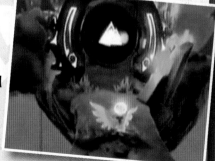

ACCESS OF LOCATION

EASY

HARD

ALL AT SEA

FLYNN'S FABLES

In some parts of Skylands – the bad parts, mostly – there's a big demand for the horns of certain creatures who kick around the place. The horns are used to make ornaments, hats, and . . . er . . . pointy stuff, then sold to the highest bidder. It's a nasty business, and no-one ever bothers to ask the poor creatures if they're using their horns before they lop them off and sell them.

Most of the time it's sky pirates who go around doing the horn-chopping, and there was once a really nasty bunch who stole more horns than anyone else. They prided themselves on being the best horn-thieves in all of Skylands, and everything from baby bulls to ancient dragons would tremble at the very mention of their name.

Once, while out scouring Skylands for more horns to harvest, the pirates stumbled upon a creature asleep on the shore. They thought they'd hit the jackpot. Not only did the sleeping dude have a horn on his head, he had horns on his tail too. Hey, even his teeth looked like horns!

They managed to take him on board their ship without waking him up, then tied him down and set to work chopping off his horns. But before they could even begin to saw, the creature woke up and . . . well, unfortunately for them, it was Slobber Tooth. Slobber Tooth, in case you were wondering, doesn't take too kindly to being woken up. And he's not exactly a big fan of pirates, either. Especially not pirates who go around stealing horns.

He tore free of the ropes like they were spider webs, then set about showing those pirates what his horns were designed for. The pirates' howls and screams were heard for miles in every direction, but Slobber Tooth was just getting warmed up.

Not having any wings, Slobber wasn't too keen on the idea of taking off into the sky in an old creaky pirate ship. So, before the pirates had even left the ground, Slobber started punching a few holes in the hull of the ship. Try flying with a ship full of holes, pirates! (It can't be done. I should know. I've tried it.) Slobber Tooth wandered happily off, knowing those pirates' days of harvesting horns were well and truly over!

HUGO'S NOTES

MOLEKIN MINER MEMOIRS

The Molekin people can be spotted all over Skylands, but they're most often found working underground, mining for everything from precious gems to fossil fuels. Unfortunately, they're very short-sighted and this occasionally leads to accidents.

Here's an extract from the diary of one Molekin Miner, following a cave-in that left him and his colleagues trapped underground. It's fascinating reading.

DAY 1
Things are going well so far. We've burrowed into a wide cave that's rich with minerals! Looks like it's our lucky day! What could possibly go wrong?

DAY 2
The cave has collapsed on us. It wasn't my fault, honest! How was I to know that sitting on that button would trigger a huge explosion? I mean, yes, someone had written 'Warning, this button will trigger a huge explosion' next to it, but they hadn't done it very clearly, and my eyesight has never been great, so it's hardly my fault. Still, at least no-one got hurt. Except Scrape and Burrow, obviously. No-one has seen them since things went **BOOM!**

DAY 3

Still no sign of Scrape or Burrow, although we did find Scrape's hard hat. Or a bit of it, anyway. We took a vote today and have decided to try digging our way out through the collapsed part of the cave. After all, it can't exactly make things any worse!

DAY 4

It made things worse. The good news is, we found Scrape and Burrow. The bad news is another bit of the cave fell on them and we've lost them again. Still, easy come easy go, I suppose. We're all starting to get worried now. We're completely trapped and air is running out. I'm starving, too. I may even have to eat you, my precious diary, if we don't get out soon.

DAY 5

We had a game of I-Spy today to pass the time. It turns out it's not a very fun game when it's pitch dark and you can't see anything. Still, I won! At least I think I did.

DAY 6

We managed to dig out Scrape and Burrow! Sadly, they then fell down a crack in the ground that no-one had noticed. We can hear them shouting about something or other, so they sound OK. Just a bit angry.

DAY 7

Tried eating a rock. It didn't go well.

DAY 8

My teeth hurt.

DAY 9

We're free! It turns out Scrape and Burrow were trying to tell us they'd found a way out! All we had to do was climb down the hole in the ground, burrow a few hundred metres, then climb up through a volcano spout! I'm writing this from the very top of the volcano, having just climbed free! Hang on . . . what's that rumbling sound?

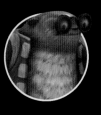

STONE-COLD RIB-TICKLERS

Being a Rock Golem, it seems quite fitting that Prism Break should be among the most stony-faced of all the Skylanders. He appears to find nothing funny, and although the other Skylanders have tried time and time again to make him laugh, they've yet to make him crack so much as a smile.

Then again, it's no wonder he doesn't laugh if the jokes below are the best they could come up with . . .

Q. What did the boy volcano say to the girl volcano?

A. I lava you!

Q. What did Bash want to be before he became a Skylander?

A. A rock star!

Q. What's Scorp's favourite game?

A. Ten pin bouldering!

Q. Why did Bash take Flashwing to the quarry?

A. He wanted to get a little boulder!

Q. Where do lazy Earth Elementals spend their days?

A. Lying around in their bedrock!

Q. Why does a space rock taste better than an earth rock?

A. Because it's a little meteor!

Q. How do you send Crusher to sleep?

A. Rock him!

Q. What is big, green and eats rocks?

A. A big green rock-eater!

TEST OF STRENGTH

Pretty much all the Skylanders have got some major muscles going on, even if they don't look like it. I mean, you might think Pop Thorn is just a cute little puff-ball, but that guy packs a serious punch. Trust me, I've felt it. But that's another story . . .

FLYNN'S FABLES

This story is about Doom Stone, and the time that he and Terrafin decided to find out which of them was the strongest.

So in one corner you had Doom Stone, a guy carved from the hardest rock in Skylands, then brought to life with magic. And in the other corner was Terrafin, a Dirt Shark with a nasty bite and a gift for punching people really hard in the head. The battle was on!

Now, these guys are friends, so they didn't want to fight one another. They decided they would each give a demonstration of their strength and let the other Skylanders decide who was toughest.

Terrafin started by lifting an enormous boulder above his head. Doom Stone replied by lifting the boulder with just one hand. But Terrafin wasn't done yet. While Doom Stone was still holding the rock, Terrafin lifted him up, so he was lifting both Doom and the boulder at once!

It looked like it was game over for Doom Stone, until he jumped down and snatched Terrafin up in one hand, and lifted the boulder with the other. Then, to the amazement of everyone (especially Terrafin), he began juggling! He was tossing the rock and the Dirt Shark up in the air and catching them, over and over again, until it looked like Terrafin might throw up!

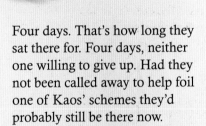

The Skylanders decided it was too close to call on who was strongest, so Master Eon, hanging around in spirit form, suggested Terrafin and Doom Stone try arm-wrestling. The two friends sat opposite one another, locked hands, and heaved with all their might.

Four days. That's how long they sat there for. Four days, neither one willing to give up. Had they not been called away to help foil one of Kaos' schemes they'd probably still be there now.

I guess we'll never know which of them is the strongest, but it's just lucky for them that they didn't get me involved in the competition. I'd have wiped the floor with both of them!

BOOM!

RUBBLE ROUSER'S ROCKY RECIPES

Rubble Rouser brings many things to the Skylanders, including might, courage and teeth that can chew through stone. Although his diet consists largely of boulders and bits of old brick, Rubble Rouser assures me he is something of a whizz in the kitchen. Here are just a few of the recipes he has recently offered to whip up for us.

ROCK CAKES

This old family recipe was given to me by my grandmother, shortly before a mountain fell on her. The cakes should be crunchy, with a crunchier aftertaste.

INGREDIENTS:

Rocks (small)
Low-fat oil (optional)

METHOD:

1. Pre-heat oven to 350F/180C.
2. Brush rocks with low-fat oil (optional) and place in the oven.
3. Wait as long as you want. It doesn't really matter.
4. Take them out.
5. Eat.

GRAVELAX

This classic recipe is a big hit at dinner parties, and is guaranteed to take guests' breath away. Usually because they're choking.

INGREDIENTS:
Gravel (or small stone chips, if gravel not available)
150g rock salt (optional)

METHOD:
1. Spread the gravel on a tray or large slab.
2. Sprinkle lightly with rock salt (optional).
3. Eat.

BOULDER SOUP

This hearty soup makes a tasty lunch, but add a handful of grit or pebbles and it can be transformed into a filling main meal.

INGREDIENTS:
A boulder (large)
Water (optional)

METHOD:
1. Get a boulder.
2. Put it in water (optional).
3. Eat.

DEFINITELY DO NOT TRY ANY OF THESE AT HOME!

EARTH:
ELEMENTS UNITE

The most solid and dependable of all the Elements that make up the Core of Light, Earth interacts with the other Elements in some very unique ways.

WEAKNESS

Althought its robustness makes Earth a force to be reckoned with, it is not without its flaws. It is at a disadvantage when facing the Air Element, and when this happens Earth Skylanders must be careful not to get blown away.

HOW EARTH ENTWINES WITH THE OTHER ELEMENTS

FIRE

Rock plus heat equals unstoppable molten lava

AIR

Combines with wind to cause deadly sandstorms

LIFE

Earth's nurturing soil allows Life to grow

MAGIC

Gives Magic some extra grit

TECH

Earth's metals and minerals give Tech its power

UNDEAD

Dark underground is the perfect Undead domain

WATER

Causes villain-devouring mudslides

FAREWELL!

Well, there we have it. Another Element guide is done and dusted. I hope it helped, although you may still have some questions, like "Flynn, how did you get to be so clever?" or "Are you as handsome in real life as you look in your pictures?" To those questions I reply, "I've always been this clever," and "Yes I am."

Good luck with your adventuring, and if you see that pesky Kaos out there, give him a spinning dash attack from me!

It's a miracle! I can scarcely believe it! Flynn is actually correct about something. I never thought I'd see the day. This is indeed the end of this guide, and I sincerely hope you've been paying attention. The information on these pages will help keep you alive (unless you try out Rubble Rouser's recipes, that is) so if you think you've missed anything at all, then go back and read again. Or read my bits again, at least. It's probably best you skip out Flynn's sections entirely.

Farewell, Portal Master. And good luck.

TWO MORE ELEMENTS, IN THE BAG!